Fleeing the Beast:
How to Find Your Authentic Self

BETSY HOUDE

Copyright © 2018 Betsy Houde

All rights reserved.

ISBN-13:
978-1720668558

ISBN-10:
1720668558

DEDICATION

Heartfelt thanks to Peter and Jane for your unconditional love and many life lessons. And to the rest of my extended family and friends for your patience and support as I travel on this journey.

COVER ART

I painted the cover painting, lovingly entitled the Flying Crone, while at a week-long inspirational painting workshop at the Omega Institute in Rhinebeck, New York, June 2004 (www.processarts.com). Facilitated by Stewart Cubley of The Painting Experience, San Francisco, CA, the workshop challenged its participants to go beyond our wildest dreams and inhibitions to tap in to the passion in our soul.

A catharsis for me, I had no idea that I had somehow adopted the "crone" identity over my 40+ years. The vulnerable young woman flying on a summer's night that I began painting, morphed into the old crone, determined to escape the clutches of the wild beast fastened to her ankles. As I painted, the wrinkles appeared, her lovely dress became frayed, and I could see a side of myself that I had never known.

Thank you family and friends for giving me the courage to put my soul on public display—not only through my art but through sharing my story. May we all have the courage to explore our demons and love ourselves just the same.

-- Betsy

ACKNOWLEDGMENTS

This book never would have happened if not for the encouragement of my new awesome photographer friend Kristin Hardwick. After I complained about having too many ideas of things I wanted to accomplish in life, she challenged me to take the first step. Thanks, too, to Jane Freund, Susan Nelson and Beth Sheehan for your helpful feedback and for the extra boost of confidence when I needed it most. I am hopeful that readers will find humor and wisdom in my journey, and find their own strength in adversity.

CONTENTS

	Introduction	1
1	Getting Started	3
2	Meeting Your Child Self	7
3	Nice Girls CAN Get Mad	11
4	Giving Up Your Turtle Shell	16
5	Letting Others Define You	20
6	The Burger King Ball Pit-- A Metaphor for Life	25
7	Is HELP a 4-Letter Word?	29
8	Never Work Harder Than Your Client	33
9	Unleashing My Inner Control Freak	37
10	Do You Know What You're Really Saying?	41
11	One-Sided Friendships	44
12	The Joy Of Ancestors	47
13	Reclaim Your Power and Give It Away	50

INTRODUCTION

Can you imagine having 1,000 candles of love and light inside that you want to give to the world? For many years I've felt messages bubbling up from inside me, but never had the confidence to share them with the world... only with family and close friends. Once I stopped allowing negative influences to "blow out my candles", the floodgates of that love and light have opened up, and I feel compelled to share messages with anyone that is open to listening! If any of these messages and accompanying challenge activities save you the countless days of stress, self-doubt and inner turmoil that I experienced in my journey, then it's all been worth it!

I love the image of the beast. I took an intuitive painting workshop years ago, and the beautiful painting of me flying across the night sky became a tattered crone with a beast holding me back from flying toward the light. The beast can be inside of us, pressing on our shoulders, hiding under the bed... to me, it's all of the negative energies and influences that we have allowed into our lives accidentally or on purpose over the years. This book is about fleeing the beast to tap into your beautiful, authentic self, and learning how to wrap yourself in love and still have plenty left for those around you.

I can't begin to count the number of people with whom I've shared life lessons to save them the time and anguish I experienced over the years – my daughter, her friends, my nieces, step kids, employees, Rotary friends, and random young professionals throughout greater Nashua, New Hampshire. Thanks for encouraging me, for insisting I'd be selfish to keep this learning all to myself and helping me tap into my inner light to let this book flow.

May this book challenge and inspire you, make you laugh and bring you to tears. It's meant to be savored over time, and give you gentle nudges to move forward on your path when you might feel stuck. If it does any or all of that, then my job is done and this has been a life well-lived.

Wishing you all the best on your journey!

1 GETTING STARTED

My journey began the day my brother died. For almost two years prior, my 4-year-old self bounced around to family friends' houses during numerous doctor's appointments, chemo treatments and surgeries. I only have snippets of memories about that time, but it shaped the next 40 years of my life. No one ever talked about their pain. It never occurred to anyone that a 6-year-old kid needed someone to talk to. His death was dubbed, "Charlie's birthday in heaven", and I learned to never bring it up again. Every year, we'd shuffle into a Mass said in his honor, but there was no sharing of stories, photos, and the like. The unspoken message was, "Don't make waves", and that meant don't talk about Charlie.

Mom became active in the American Cancer Society as a way to channel her grief, I guess. I channeled my grief into behaving. Being "Good Little Betsy" was an easy task. I was always compliant, got A's on my report card and did my chores without complaint. Dad called me the "Lap Sneaker", because he'd be reading the newspaper after a long day at work, and I would somehow slip under the newspaper and snuggle on his lap. I craved affection and attention and always did my best in order to get it. Although my older sister and I would squabble from time to time, it was never to the point that our parents had to intervene.

Baby brother was born almost two years later. I was so excited to have a new toy to play with, and was emotionally rewarded for being a great little helper. My identity formed around trying to earn approval for being well-behaved, a good student and a good helper. The more attention I showered on my brother, the more I was emotionally fed with his positive response and for giving my Mom a respite from his needs.

My parents' communication style was pretty typical for the time — they never disagreed about anything in front of us or engaged in any kind of meaningful conversation with us. Maybe they talked about important things after we were in bed, but it was never apparent. They both came from "children shall be seen and not heard" parents, which seems to have played itself out with us. Hence, I didn't know how to NOT be good. I didn't know that I would still be loved if I misbehaved. My self-esteem was so closely tied to not making mistakes that I never allowed myself that freedom.

Fast forward into adolescence and young adulthood, and it's not surprising that I struggled with low self-esteem. I was one of those people that had no idea that I was attractive or a "catch". I was never popular, but hung on the fringes of all of the social groups in high school since I was nice. No one was ever threatened by my intelligence or work ethic, so I was invited along. It was pretty convenient that I was the first in my friend group to get my driver's license and have access to a car, because I liked being needed and it made sure that I got invited places...

I willingly gave 100% of my heart and my energy to others, without ever asking for or expecting anything in return. The people I dated — and subsequently married — loved the fact that I was sweet and compliant and never made waves. I'd been brainwashed that nice girls don't get mad and was the ultimate people pleaser. I didn't know how to acknowledge or express negative emotions... it was a foreign concept.

Everything shifted for me when I was awarded a national fellowship to develop my leadership skills and matched with a mentor. She challenged me to do a strategic plan on myself. It forced me to "go deep" and assess all of my personal strengths, weaknesses opportunities and threats. It wasn't easy to acknowledge that at my core, I was a people-pleasing doormat. I never put any time into identifying my needs, hopes and dreams because I was so invested in helping my loved ones achieve theirs. It's been a long and powerful journey on the road to meet myself, and I am in love with the person I found. I urge you to learn from my struggles to save yourself the time and anguish. Please take the time to complete the challenge activities that resonate with you in this book. Please dig around in your soul to confront any hurtful or harmful messages you've carried with you for your entire life. Now is your chance to decide whether to keep those beastly messages or kick them to the curb. Letting those negative messages go is empowering and freeing and just might change your life. I often say, "If I can pick up one new nugget, then my time has been worth it." May you find your own nugget of wisdom somewhere in my story.

CHALLENGE ACTIVITY #1

I had an ex that would blow up at my daughter and me when he was having a bad day and we were convenient. At a young age, I needed to teach her how to separate what was hers to deal with and what to let go, because I was afraid that his moods would permeate her soul. (Fast forward— that's the reason I finally gave up and left my second marriage.) Here's what I would say to her: "If you did something you weren't supposed to do, or didn't do something you were supposed to do... you need to deal with it. If not, you have to let it go... it's not about you."

This equates to my definition of the "beast"—the attitude and energy manifested in someone outside of us; however, the messages could easily have been internalized if we weren't careful. For me, it's one thing to hear a harmful or hurtful message in my brain, but another when I let it soak into my heart, because that's where I draw my energy. Think about the unhelpful or negative messages you've heard from people you care about and write them down in the chart. Let it flow without judgment.

	Message	It is stuck in your brain?	It is stuck in your heart?
1			
2			
3			
4			
5			

Once your list is complete, go back and try to figure out whether those messages got stuck in your head, or found their way to your heart. Are they valid? What can you let go of?

	How does this impact me today?	How can I let it go?
1		
2		
3		
4		
5		

Make a commitment to yourself to work through these unhealthy messages. Remember that change often happens slowly, and you need to be patient with yourself. If you're carrying multiple messages that are negatively impacting your life, identify one or two that may be priorities for you. It might make sense to pick one of the easier ones to let go of first! You don't want to get discouraged choosing the most difficult challenge as your first attempt to let go.

I commit the following to myself: _____

_____

_____

_____

_____

_____

_____

_____

_____

_____

_____

_____

_____

_____

2 MEETING YOUR CHILD SELF

I am my own worst critic. While I'm a lot nicer to myself today than I used to be, I still have high expectations. There's a concept that resonates with me that we each have a child living inside of us. We get to assign whatever age we want to that child. It really makes sense if you think about it!

I joke with people today that I am a 12-year-old trapped in an adult body. It's hard being responsible, serving as a role model to others, parenting and such. Even though I went to graduate school for a degree in counseling and my professor talked about the "inner child", he never pushed us to identify and embrace ours. I was 30 when I made the effort to "meet" my inner child. I found myself unexpectedly single with a new baby trying to figure out why I wasn't good enough for my husband to choose me (and our daughter) instead of someone else. It was a pretty blurry time in my life but somehow I got the inspiration to write a letter from my adult self to my inner child. At the time, my "Little Betsy" was six years old, the same age I was when my brother died.

CHALLENGE ACTIVITY #2

When you picture yourself as a child, what age are you? Are you a toddler, young school age, pre-teen, teen? Try to go with the first image that pops in your head and don't over think it. Consider the various struggles your little self might have been experiencing at that age and the kinds of messages that could be helpful to someone in those circumstances.

Now close your eyes and step outside of your little self and be your fabulous adult-mentor self. What would you say to your little self? Children deserve to be loved. Our inner children deserve to be loved. It's up to us to learn how to meet our own needs for self-love. Check out the sample for ideas to get started, and then write your Little Self a letter in the space provided below.

> *Dear _____,*
>
> *I know that you're struggling with _____ and it's okay... I see how hard you try every day to do your best, and that's all you can do. It's not your job to have to _____ and it's not fair that _____.*
>
> *I'm so proud of you for _____ and for how you're handling yourself. It's okay to reach out for help, and I'm always here if you need me. I won't let anything happen to you...*

You get the idea, right? Use the following space to write your own letter to your Little Self. When you're done, read your letter aloud as if you're the adult. Then read it aloud again listening to it from the perspective of your child. Allow the emotion of what you wrote to flow through you. Date your letter so you can look back at it in the future.

Date: _____

Dear _____,

_____

_____

_____

_____

_____

_____

_____

_____

_____

_____

_____

What surfaced for you that was unexpected? _____

Did this exercise trigger any emotions in you? If so, what got stirred up? _____

Honoring and acknowledging your inner child is so important because he or she relies on us to keep them safe and ensure they are loved. Did any surprising harmful or hurtful messages get stirred up during your letter that might need to be explored more fully? Please list the ones that seem like they're holding you back the most:

Message	Action Step to help you move beyond it

What commitment can you make to yourself (and your inner child) to take action? Add your thoughts below:

_____

_____

_____

_____

_____

_____

_____

3 NICE GIRLS CAN GET MAD

I grew up in an era where "nice girls don't get mad"... and "if you can't say anything nice, don't say anything at all". My parents never fought (at least in front of us), so I never learned how to stand up for myself or to express anger appropriately. The road was long between "doormat" and "empowered woman", but I'm happy to offer a few strategies that might help you on your journey.

When I get mad, I get calm... focused... and my voice actually gets quieter, but firm. The people that know me really well know that I'm far more dangerous when I'm quiet than if I'm blustering about something.

I was married to a guy that would try to provoke me to stoop to his level, because he couldn't stand the fact that I was in control of my emotions when he was a red-faced screamer. The high road is always a much better place to be, and far more productive. If someone is trying to provoke you, just stop and breathe. Count to ten if you need to. It's perfectly fine to simply say, "I'm way too angry to have this conversation right now. I'm going to calm down." And then walk away... go sit in your car, lock your door. Do whatever you need to do to have some time to be by yourself and reflect on how you really feel about what just happened and how you want to respond. That extra bit of time can help you move past typical triggers that set you off, and give you the time and space to respond differently.

Also ask yourself, "What am I truly mad about?" Is it that the dishes weren't done, or that you feel disrespected in your relationship? You'll get further down the road to self-awareness if you can ask yourself the tough questions. Do I really care about this? Is this a battle worth fighting? What old stuff is getting triggered in me to elicit this kind of anger?

Keep in mind that it's totally acceptable to express your displeasure about the thing that JUST happened, but bringing up old stuff is never okay. That generalizes the issue and brings up "dirty laundry". Be angry that s/he was late, forgot something, left a mess, etc. (pick your pet peeve), but as soon as you throw in the "You ALWAYS......" you've crossed a line, and it's not a good line to cross.

Life is a constant learning opportunity, and it's incumbent on each of us to dig deep and be as authentic as we can. I had an example recently that shows how my process is constantly evolving.

I hired a wonderful counselor recently to work with teens in a school setting. During the interview, she impressed me with her heart, spunk, passion for kids and interest in our mission. But I couldn't get past the fact that she had bright pink hair. I asked her outright how committed she was to her hair color if she was really interested in the job. She wanted the job badly enough that she readily agreed to tone it way down. She was the perfect choice and a great fit. Fast forward six months and I missed our weekly staff meeting. My admin pulled me aside and told me that the counselor was relieved I wasn't there because her hair was bright blue. My first reaction was, "Are you f'ing kidding me?"

After much muttering and shaking my head in disbelief, I began to dig deep. Why did I care? What does this mean? What do I say or do? I'm the boss/leader/role model, so my reaction and subsequent action would be dissected by everyone. I decided that I was relieved I missed the staff meeting, because I might have blurted out something totally embarrassing to myself or to the counselor, and needed time to process. Next, since the school district contracts with us for this service I opted to call the principal to ask about their dress code policy and whether that look was acceptable for employees or not. I decided to base my next move on his response. He said, "I don't care, as long as she's good with the kids."

Now I was stuck because the school didn't care, but I cared deeply. The principal took away my opportunity to blame him for my response. I needed to figure out why I was so angry and figure out how to respond. I knew that the counselor was too sweet a person to have it be a giant "F-you" to me or to the agency, so I wasn't going to go there... After much soul searching, I came to the realization that since we are such a small organization (12 staff), I consider every single employee a reflection of me personally. I'd spent more than 20 years growing the reputation of this organization and I didn't want to lose our credibility. I don't have an issue with expressive hair for my children, friends or peers, but as egocentric as it sounds, this counselor was a direct reflection of ME. She knew it wasn't going to go over well and had basically spent two weeks hiding from me. Sadly, she was petrified that I'd fire her, which never even occurred to me.

I guess there are at least two lessons here. My counselor basically created her own hell, adding two weeks of unnecessary stress to her life by waiting for my reaction. I told her that I wished she'd texted a picture of her new color right away with a "Yikes! This wasn't what I was going for!" and we could've crafted a plan together to fix it somehow or hope it rinsed out fast. She was most worried that she had disappointed me and that I "would hate her for it", which broke my heart. That brought me right back to my days as a group home child care worker, where I could confidently tell her that I loved HER and thought she was awesome, but I didn't like her hair. It's so important to separate out the person from their behavior... It was kind of funny how she put herself through far more anguish than I ever would have as her boss. During our discussion, I shared with her how I wrestled with the situation myself trying to figure out why I cared so much. I laughed with her about the power of karma, and sent her off with a hug to be her amazing self.

CHALLENGE ACTIVITY #3

Think about your own style. Do you tend to stuff your anger inside more often than you let it flow uncensored or vice versa? Look back on your life and pick a situation where you could've expressed your anger rather than stuffed it, or could've tempered your anger to get to a more satisfying resolution instead of unleashing it full force. Jot down your story below:

_____

_____

_____

_____

_____

_____

_____

_____

_____

I find it helpful to explore the "worst case scenario" to give me courage when I'm stuffing my feelings. As you review your story above, what would you have liked to say or do instead of what you did/didn't say or do? Brainstorm a bunch of worst case scenarios that could have played out if you took your preferred path. It's helpful to be prepared for any eventuality as you're deciding how you want to proceed. It's also helpful to realize that most of the worst case scenarios are never going to happen, which will help reduce stress.

Explore your options:

Option 1: What could you have said/done differently? _____

_____

_____

_____

_____

What's the worst thing that could have happened if you took that route? _____

_____

_____

_____

_____

_____

Option 2: What could you have said/done differently? _____

_____

_____

_____

_____

What's the worst thing that could have happened if you took that route? _____

_____

_____

_____

_____

Did you have any personal realizations as a result of this exercise? _____

_____

_____

_____

_____

_____

_____

_____

_____

_____

_____

What commitment can you make to yourself about embracing anger in a healthy way as you go forward?

_____

_____

_____

_____

_____

Choose another time when you stuffed your anger instead of expressing it and go through the exercise again. Include any additional thoughts below:

_____

_____

_____

_____

_____

4 GIVING UP YOUR TURTLE SHELL

Although I consider myself empowered, I'm also conflict averse! When I was a kid, I'd cry when my Dad raised his voice with my sister. Looking back, I think they were just debating politics, but their tones of voice always overwhelmed me. Hence, I tend to retreat into myself when people argue or when I'm in a conversation with someone getting loud.

When I worked in a group home for children and teens, we attended a training on nonviolent crisis intervention. A key point was when a kid is screaming at you, wait until they stop yelling to breathe, and then restate your expectation. Staying calm is key. Imagine yourself in that scenario, quietly restating your expectation. "I'm sorry you're mad, but it's not an option...". If the other party in your argument thinks that they can yell or bully you into submission — and you give in to the pressure — you've lost a lot of ground that could take weeks or months to rebuild. Some people like to push our buttons to see how we're going to react. Be in charge of yourself! Eventually the button pushers won't get any satisfaction out of not riling you up and will go elsewhere.

Nowadays, when I want to confront someone, I often use the strategy of being "confused". For example, "I'm really confused that you just said _____, when five minutes ago you said _____. I thought we agreed on _____." It's an in-your-face confrontation and sounds much nicer than, "You have no idea what you're talking about!" or calling them an idiot.

I prefer to present myself in a one-down position in those cases to make my point — and hopefully resolve it — than to elicit a defensive response in someone else. You can also use the phrase, "Help me understand..." if that language is more comfortable. "Help me understand how this is going to help..."

You can also use the same strategy for actions that were done or left undone. "I'm so confused! You told me you'd be home by 5 to walk the dog, and I got home at 7 and you still weren't back..." That kind of approach allows the other person to digest what you're saying without jumping straight to defensiveness. Maybe there was a car accident or crisis, and if you start with a loud, angry demeanor, you might miss something important. You might inadvertently discourage the person from talking about things that are bothering them if you regularly appear confrontational or judgmental.

An employee recently complained to me about a staff member (with no authority over her) who commented multiple times about her being late for work. It was none of the other employee's business, but my staff member, out of habit, started explaining what happened to make her late. She was annoyed with herself for automatically responding and looking to me for advice. I suggested that she reframe the entire conversation to make it positive. I encouraged her to respond something like, "Thank you so much for worrying about me! It's all good..." and then to walk away. I'll include more about the challenges of giving away your own personal power later.

CHALLENGE ACTIVITY #4

Are there times where you freeze up, knowing that you have a valid point about something, but have trouble getting it out? Often, the best responses come to me long after the issue at hand, denying me the opportunity for my perfect come back... This exercise is to help you develop some language and comfort with speaking up rather than slipping back into your own turtle shell. Write down a few situations below where you felt stuck or powerless in the first column.

Situation	Response to Convey My Opinion

As you re-read them, think about the wide array of phrases you could use to convey your opinion. Having some statements at the ready will help give you a place to start expressing yourself in difficult situations more comfortably.

Samples: *We're going to have to agree to disagree on that point.*
I can't support that way of thinking.
I'm not comfortable with the direction you're recommending.
That's an interesting point.
Thank you for your input.

Notice that these phrases are not diminishing the other person in any way, but clearly stating that you have an opinion about the topic that needs further exploration.

What will be the hardest part of starting to "stick your neck out" to share an opinion? _____

_____

_____

_____

_____

_____

_____

How can you overcome that? _____

_____

_____

_____

_____

_____

_____

What commitment will you make to yourself to start practicing this? _____

_____

_____

_____

_____

_____

_____

_____

Please add any additional thoughts below: _____

_____

_____

_____

_____

_____

_____

5 LETTING OTHERS DEFINE YOU

Author Barbara DeAngelis wrote about two reasons why people love. Although I read her book, *Are You the One for Me?* several years ago, the notion really stuck with me. She believes that one reason people love is to fill themselves up. The other reason (paraphrased) is because you're so overflowing with love for yourself that it spills on to the people around you. I was baffled by the second reason people love. Isn't that selfish? Shouldn't I be giving love to others before myself?

This conundrum became the turning point for me to stop being a people pleaser at age 42. All I could do was laugh at myself. I worked in human services, I cared deeply about how other people felt about things... all at the expense of myself and my own identity. I loved others in order to fill myself up. In doing so, I realized that I was allowing other people to define me, based on whether they liked or didn't like whatever I said or did, and whomever I was at my core.

That's such a bunch of crap and so demeaning to myself, but up until that point, I hadn't stepped outside of myself to know that was unhealthy and to see how I'd fallen into that trap.

No wonder past partners hadn't respected me! I basically didn't respect myself enough to have strong boundaries... to say NO when I wanted or needed to. People pleasing had become such a huge part of my identity. It was scary to contemplate how I'd be received when I stopped pleasing others in an effort to better love myself.

My first challenge happened on a 4th of July. I literally sat in the parking lot by myself outside of our local fireworks show for about 10 minutes debating in my head, "Do I really want to go to the fireworks? Do I care?" I'd go every year with my family, but now that my time was my own, did I really want to? After much internal struggle and self-talk, I decided, "Hell no!", and went to the movies instead. I'd never bothered to think about my preferences before. I was always easy going and accommodating, but lo and behold, I have opinions I never knew about! The next part of my journey was about discovering those opinions. I have become opinionated!

CHALLENGE ACTIVITY #5

Think about your relationships and how you interact with the world. Are you a person that gives love to fill yourself up or are you one that has enough self-love to let it flow over you and spread onto the people around you? Share your thoughts below:

_____

_____

_____

_____

_____

_____

_____

_____

_____

_____

_____

_____

_____

The book *The Four Agreements* by Don Miguel Ruiz is one of my all-time favorites. One of the agreements is "Take Nothing Personally". While easier said than done, I believe this strongly relates to having enough love for oneself — and thereby confidence in yourself — to understand that other people's reactions may not have anything to do with you! Perhaps the other person is having a bad day, something you said triggered a memory or emotion for the other, and so forth.

As long as your action or comment comes from a place of love, you can't be responsible (or accountable) for how the other person receives the action or comment.

Think about a time when you said or did something that another person took completely out of context. Did your comment or action come from a place of love? Did you beat yourself up about the other person's reaction? Jot down your thoughts below:

_____
_____
_____
_____
_____
_____
_____
_____
_____

Have there been times when you're the one that reacted in an angry, upset or blaming way when someone said or did something that came from a place of love? Jot down your thoughts below:

_____
_____
_____
_____
_____
_____

What do you think got churned up that lead to your over-the-top reaction? _____

Is that wound still festering now or have you resolved it with the other person? _____

What steps can you take to ensure you're more in control of your emotions going forward? _____

Did anything else get churned up thinking about these nuggets that you need to address going forward? Share your thoughts below and identify ways you could address them.

6 THE BURGER KING BALL PIT— A METAPHOR FOR LIFE

While a story about the Burger King ball pit may seem silly at first glance, it has become a powerful metaphor for my life!

When my daughter was three, she wanted to play in the BK's ball pit, but a little boy was blocking the entrance. We went up to him together and said, "Excuse me... please move because she is allowed to play here, too." The boy reluctantly moved and she went inside the play structure. They were the only two kids in the area.

Less than two minutes later, she came out crying telling me the boy had pinched her. A million thoughts raced through my head while I was consoling her, and I was obviously angry on her behalf. As I pondered our options, a lightbulb went off in my head.

Between her tears I said to her, "You were trying to be nice, but now you're mad and crying. That's not fair. We need to figure out how to switch it around so HE'S the one mad and crying since he's not being nice."

In 3-year-old speak, we processed options that would make sure that HE was the one mad and crying instead. The two options we came up with was to find his mother and tell her, or to go find the "Burger King lady" and let her know what happened. I don't actually remember how it was resolved — she probably wanted to leave at that point — but the message stuck with us and we've since applied it to so many life situations!

When was the last time that you were trying to be nice and wound up mad and crying instead? With your kids? Work? Relationships? You've got to find a way to switch up the energy.

I shared this story last year with my frantic co-worker. Her 13-year-old son took the bus home for the very first time and was supposed to call her as soon as he got home. She was calling every family member she could find because he wasn't answering his phone. I told her that she could leave work early, but predicted that he would blow her off with a, "Mom, I'm FINE! You worry too much." After sharing my Burger King metaphor, we devised a plan...

We strategized that she would call the non-emergency number of their local police department to explain the situation and ask if someone was available to stop by the house to check on him. Before she activated that plan, her son finally did call her (almost an hour late). In pure dramatic fashion, she exclaimed, "Oh! I was so worried, I called the police and asked them to check on you!" He totally freaked out and started crying thinking the police were coming to the house. It all resolved quickly. The Mom got the reaction she was hoping for, and every Friday at 2:28pm since, her phone rings with a report that her son is home safely.

It was so much more satisfying than if she had rushed home to find her 13-year-old eating Doritos on the couch making fun of her for feeling stressed. The energy shifted to exactly where it needed to be.

CHALLENGE ACTIVITY #6

Shifting energy when you're the one being nice and wind up "mad and crying" requires creativity! If you're really angry, it would be wise to take a short time out before devising your plan, since you want to make sure that the "punishment fits the crime" so to speak.

Think about a time when you were attempting to be nice to your child, partner, co-worker, sibling, etc., and instead wound up right back in the BK's ball pit mad and crying because you were being disrespected, taken advantage of, and so forth. Jot it down below:

_____
_____
_____
_____
_____
_____
_____

Brainstorm a couple of scenarios that you could have implemented to shift the energy back to where it belonged rather than allow yourself to remain mad and crying when you were simply trying to be nice. After each one, add your thoughts on "What's the worst thing that could happen?" as a result of your response, to ensure that you're making the best decision for yourself at the time. (There's more about the "worst thing" process under Nice Girls CAN Get Mad.)

Creative Response	Worst Thing That Could Happen

Do you find yourself "mad and crying" pretty often when you're trying to be nice? Jot down a couple of more scenarios below to help solidify this way of shifting energy. It works, and the more you practice, the easier it becomes!

1) _____

Creative Response	Worst Thing That Could Happen

2) _____

_____

_____

_____

_____

_____

_____

_____

Creative Response	Worst Thing That Could Happen

Use this space for any additional thoughts: _____

_____

_____

_____

7 IS HELP A 4-LETTER WORD?

A few years ago, I read that it's selfish NOT to ask for help. I wish I remembered the book so I could cite the author, but that notion really stuck with me. I never liked asking for help because I didn't want to be a burden to people. Did it mean that I was somehow deficient if I couldn't handle something myself and needed help? Was that an unhealthy message left over from childhood?

The thought that it's selfish to NOT ask for help really bothered me since I work with a bunch of helpers, and have been a helper all of my adult life. We want and need people to ask for help from us in order to do our job. I've always known that picking up the phone and asking for help from the nonprofit where I work is the hardest part, and we strive to be welcoming and supportive. However...

When it's our turn to reach out for help, all of a sudden, it's difficult... embarrassing... unnecessary... burdensome. We'd rather struggle alone than ask someone to help. Think about it!

The author basically said that by NOT asking for help, we are putting ourselves in a one-up position with others. It's selfish! WE get to feel the gift of being needed, yet don't allow others in our lives the chance to be needed by us. It feels so good to believe that others find our help valuable, yet we deny that same gift to others.

I can't count the number of times I was wide awake in the middle of the night, basically having conversations with God because there was no one else I felt I could talk to about whatever issue I was facing. I've been comfortable talking to friends AFTER I'd already pulled myself together, but never in the midst of a major meltdown. My style is more, "Let me tell you what happened to me last week/month/year...." rather than, "Please hug me because I'm falling apart."

Ultimately, I'd label myself a bit of an introverted loner, but I have no idea whether it's a chicken-egg theory thing. Did I become more of a loner because I didn't feel comfortable asking for help and learned to problem solve on my own? Is it because I'm a Capricorn and that sign is more independent than connected? Part of me thinks that I would love to be coddled if I'm home feeling sick. The other part would be mortified by that level of attention and I think that I'd prefer to be alone. Fortunately, I'm rarely sick so haven't had to answer that question... it's tough stuff!

CHALLENGE ACTIVITY #7

What's your style around asking for help? Are you comfortable with seeking help in the moment? Do you try to problem solve yourself and only seek help as a last resort?

Some colleagues and I conducted focus groups in our community around defining what it means to be responsible. We synthesized the feedback to mean that being responsible is about:

- *owning your actions*
- *knowing when you need help and then*
- *asking for help.*

Think about your style asking for and receiving help and include your answers below.

	Very	**Somewhat**	**Not Very**	**Not at All**
How comfortable are you asking for help for yourself for something small?				
How comfortable are you asking for help for yourself for something big?				
How comfortable are you providing help to someone else for something small?				
How comfortable are you providing help to someone else for something big?				

Do you notice any pattern in your responses that are healthy for you or unhealthy? Share your thoughts below:

_____

_____

_____

_____

Think about a time when asking for help really would have made a difference in your life, but you chose to handle it all on your own. Write it down below:

_____

_____

_____

_____

_____

In the following table, list 3 people that care about you (or should care about you by the nature of your relationship). How would they have responded if you asked for help?

Names	How would they respond to your request for help?	What's the worst thing that could happen if you ask?
1		
2		
3		

Now think about those same three people coming to YOU asking for YOUR help with something. How do you react when they ask YOU for help?

Names	How do you/would you react if they ask for help?	Why?
1		
2		
3		

Do you buy into the idea that NOT asking for help is selfish? Why or why not?

_____
_____
_____
_____
_____
_____
_____

Have any nuggets of wisdom start percolating for you after doing this exercise? Jot them down below:

_____
_____
_____
_____
_____
_____
_____
_____
_____
_____

8 NEVER WORK HARDER THAN YOUR CLIENT

I'm sure this phrase is debatable based on what occupation or industry you're referring to, but allow me to share my context. One of my professors shared this nugget, back when I was training to become a family therapist. He challenged us to consider the dynamic that could occur if I wanted something more for my therapy client than he or she wanted for themselves.

My job was to help motivate the client, to explore barriers that might be holding them back from achieving their goals, and so forth. But if I were to find myself in the role of wanting my client to be more successful — with anything — more than he or she wanted it, the whole balance gets skewed. I could wind up being angry with them rather than supportive. My job wasn't to fix things for them, but to create a space where they could find the inner strength to step up and move forward on their own.

I've shared this phrase so many times with colleagues. Hopefully this nugget will become clearer with some relevant examples.

I have the distinct pleasure of consulting with a community coalition working to reduce substance misuse and risky behavior among teens. We launched a youth video project seeking teams of teens to create public service announcements, spending hours voting on themes, locating powerful quotes to go with the themes and planning a red carpet event to honor the multitude of teen groups that were going to enter. We convinced a local foundation to give a grand prize of having the winning video produced professionally and shown at the local movie theater for a month. We were so excited! More than two dozen applications came in by the first deadline indicating that they were working on creating a video. When the submission deadline finally arrived, we noted that some teams didn't follow through, others sent us a half-hearted attempt, and others didn't turn in the required video release forms signed by parents.

The group struggled with whether we should go out of our way checking in with the youth teams to extend our submission deadline, give them a chance to improve their video, or chase parent signatures ourselves. I shared the nugget about never working harder than your client, and the fact that the real world has rules people need to follow. The planning committee decided to redesign the red carpet event and prize structure instead, to make sure the coalition got the final product it really wanted.

Do you sometimes inadvertently make life too easy for others because you're the one doing all the work? Sadly, that can be a recipe for burnout and resentment. I used to struggle with this dynamic regularly, until I found a balance between my need-to-be-needed and the reality that I was possibly being used.

Are you a parent that cleans your kid's bedroom (does their laundry, you name it), while they're watching TV? When my daughter was a 3-year-old, she started putting her own laundry away through a "store" game, where I'd sell her clean laundry for beads. It was silly and fun and she learned to take care of her own clothes. By about age 10, she handled it all herself.

If you want your loved one to get a job more than he or she wants to work, stop paying for all of their meals, phone, entertainment, etc. Life is a lot about motivation… if your effort to be kind, caring and supportive is allowing the other person to suck you dry of money, energy, and so forth, it's not a healthy balance. You need to find a way to respect yourself and shift the energy. (Go back and re-read my Burger King Ball Pit analogy and allow yourself to acknowledge that you might be mad about the pattern you've created!)

CHALLENGE ACTIVITY #8

Are there places in your life where you're working harder than your "client" – partner, sibling, parent, child, friend, co-worker in an effort to help improve THEIR lives? It's one thing if the person needs short-term support to get through an illness, and such, but I'm talking about ingrained patterns of behavior that you didn't even realize you stepped into.

I learned years ago that you can't improve your behavior at any level until you make the "unconscious conscious". You need to step back from your habits, patterns and behaviors to see where you might be short-changing yourself from living fully (and happily). It's a risk because there's no going back once you've become aware of where you got stuck, but worth the effort in the long run!

Complete the table below thinking about the key people in your life.

Name	Am I working harder on their behalf than they are?	How can I resolve this?

What, if anything, was stirred up for you as you pondered the concept? _____

_____

_____

_____

_____

_____

_____

_____

If you've identified a pattern of your behavior that needs to change, what steps can you take to make sure that you respect yourself enough to start making the change? Keep in mind that you can only change YOUR behavior, and YOUR response to someone else. You can't change anyone else… you can only set the stage for them that may lead to change… but ultimately it's their decision!

_____

_____

_____

_____

_____

_____

_____

_____

_____

Please add any additional thoughts here:

9 UNLEASHING MY INNER CONTROL FREAK

When a workshop presenter, Judy, challenged our small fellowship group to identify a personal quality that defined us, I mumbled, "Controlling bitch...". She overheard me and asked, "Why do you think that's such a bad thing?"

In an instant, Judy reframed a huge part of my self-identity into something positive! She pointed out that my preference to be in control of something was not about my ego (she'd known me for a couple of years), but was about quality assurance. That was easy for me to grasp. Of course I wanted anything I was involved with to be of good quality. I'd worked for years to earn my reputation as a nonprofit leader. I valued my time. I wanted to invest it wisely into helping to develop initiatives and people that would improve our community.

Rather than disparaging myself for being a control freak, my challenge was to embrace this part of my leadership self. Sticking one's neck out is scary, but holding back when you have a great idea to contribute is worse.

Keep in mind that my definition of being a control freak doesn't involve shoving others out of the way or dismissing other ideas. I firmly believe that a single idea, shared with another person or group, can grow into something completely amazing when you shine a light on the idea and invite others to help grow it. It's about planting seeds, seeing what ideas take hold and then nurturing them into something special.

In my work life, I find that I am either 110% invested in a project or idea, or I need to back off completely. There's no middle ground for me. I can't sit in meeting after meeting to develop an idea that I'm not invested in that I feel has little chance for success. I'm never offended if people don't like my ideas, but if I can't muster enough creative energy to be invested in the project, there are better ways to use my time. I've learned to politely decline involvement and move on without burning bridges.

I can't count the number of times one of my staff has said to me, "I'm waiting to hear back from..." with regard to a really important project. I always try to help them identify *Who cares the most about this project?* If my counselor cares more about the project than the school principal, for example, I will encourage them to take the lead and follow up by phone, in person, and so forth. People are busy! If you are expecting someone else to care more about your important thing than you do, you'll probably wind up frustrated, disappointed and way behind in your intended timeline.

I encourage my staff to bug me about something if they don't hear back from me about a pending decision. I've typically got 1,000 things on my plate, and whether we have enough funds allocated for them to attend a conference is probably not the highest priority for ME, but could have a huge impact on their need for continuing education credits, licensure, etc. Since that is far more important to them than to me, I encourage them to take control to the extent that they can. The phrase I use is, "You are your own best advocate!"

I love tropical vacations, and even better if they involve a cruise ship to get there! Hubby has learned to love them, too, but they are far more important to me. Not once in our years together has he ever said, "What do you think about going on a cruise?" I'm the researcher and planner. I take joy in hunting for the best itinerary and ship for the cost. If I waited around for him to suggest it, I'd be sun-deprived and miserable... and probably 100 years old.

CHALLENGE ACTIVITY #9

Think about your own self and how you interact with the world. Are there aspects of your life where you're overly controlling and need to let go? Are there areas where you can be more outspoken to ensure your needs are met?

Please use this space to write down any areas where you may be overly controlling in a way that is hurting your current relationships.

_____

_____

_____

_____

_____

_____

_____

_____

What changes might you make to help these relationships be more satisfying?

_____

_____

_____

_____

_____

Are there parts of your life that you tend to hold back saying or doing what you really need to be more fulfilled? Please list them below.

_____

_____

_____

_____

_____

What do you think is holding you back?

_____

_____

_____

_____

_____

What changes might you make to help you move forward?

What will be the hardest part of incorporating these changes in your life?

10 DO YOU KNOW WHAT YOU'RE REALLY SAYING?

After a tough afternoon bickering with the neighborhood kids, my then 5-year-old daughter referred to one of them as an asshole. I was totally taken aback, because I had been careful with my language around her. Stunned I responded, "Do you know what that really means?" She gave me a blank stare, so I responded, "That's the place where the poop comes out. Did you really mean to call Sammy the place where the poop comes out?" She was horrified and upset that she would say something so ugly about her friend. They were just having a bad day.

Fast forward about 20 years and my daughter is now a 5th grade teacher and overheard one of her students use a disparaging remark about someone else. "Do you know what that really means?" was her immediate response. I love it when my words come out of her mouth now that she's an adult!

I'm a firm believer in the law of what goes around comes around. Do you enjoy gossiping about others or creating drama? I identified a dynamic recently that disturbs me. I've noticed that some folks are using gossip and drama as a way to connect with other people, thus using it as the basis of forming friendships. Have we lost that much ground as a society? Building a solid friendship is about sharing what's in your heart, what you're struggling with, being authentic. It's not about a shared disdain for your job, co-worker, neighbor, etc. Those people are not true friends, and are not likely to have your back when the tough stuff comes along. Motivational speaker Jim Rohn said that we are the average of the five people we spend the most time with. Food for thought…

CHALLENGE ACTIVITY #10

With social media today, we know that the old "Sticks and stones will break my bones but names will never hurt me" is a thing of the past. Gossip is toxic and has driven numerous people to consider taking their own lives and far too many follow through. I urge you to take a detached look at your closest five relationships to help identify which people bring our your best self, and which tend to bring out your more negative character traits.

	Name	Positive energy/ uplifting	Negative energy/ brings you down	How can you shift it to be more authentic?
1				
2				
3				
4				
5				

If your list of close relationships brings you more negative than positive energy, think about people that you admire. Are there ways you can outreach to get to know these people better? It's never too late to grow your circle of friends. It's also important to realize that as you grow and mature over the years, the type of friends you need to sustain you will shift, as well. Your best drinking buddy may not be the right fit after you have a child, and so forth.

Name	What can you do to reach out?

What realizations, if any, came to you as a result of this exercise?

___

What steps do you need to take to move forward?

___

11 ONE-SIDED FRIENDSHIPS

My challenge parenting an only child was making sure she always had friends available for play dates. It took the wisdom of a 7-year-old to come up with this nugget:

"How come I'm always calling HER to come over, but she never invites ME?"

Hmmmm... that was an interesting point. It got me thinking about the concept of a "one-sided friendship". I define that as a relationship where one person feels like they are doing all of the work to keep the friendship/relationship going.

I used to be the "glue" for my two siblings and me. I was the one that always kept in touch, calling every few weeks or so, asking about how they were doing, and such. It made me feel connected to them and to their lives and to my nieces and nephew. When I'd call my Mom to chat — since I was the child that called most regularly — I would always fill her in on what everyone else was involved in to help her feel connected.

After I pondered the idea of a one-sided friendship, it got me thinking. I started to wonder how long it would take one of my siblings to reach out to ME if I wasn't doing all the work. Would they spend time thinking about me enough to reach out? Would they call to ask how I was doing? I don't remember exactly how long it took one of them to call me, but it felt like a really long time. I decided that I didn't need to be the glue anymore. I love them both and have a wonderful time when we get together, but I no longer count on those relationships to fill me up.

In her book, *The Dance of Intimacy*, Harriet Lerner, PhD, described relationships as a dance. I love the concept of the pursuer and distancer. Think about it. If one person pursues too much, the other person tends to distance. If you want to be pursued, try creating a little distance to bring the other person closer to you.

In simpler terms I am reminded of the 1972 children's book *Leave Herbert Alone* by Alma Marshak Whitney. Herbert, the cat, is tired of being approached by the eager child. He's only comfortable allowing her to engage with him after she learns to sit quietly on the porch steps. This dynamic can be visible in all kinds of relationships – with friendships, roommates, dating, and so forth.

With the busyness of today's society, people often complain that they simply didn't have time to connect. However, if they were really interested in maintaining a connection with us, I believe they would find the time. The same is true for each of us — it's our job to make an effort to reach out if we want to nurture our friendships with others.

CHALLENGE ACTIVITY #11

Take a moment to reflect on the key people in your life and think about the following questions:
- *Do you both make an effort to stay connected?*
- *Are you the one doing all of outreach or perhaps are you the one who waits for the other person to contact you?*
- *Do you tend to meet the other person halfway when trying to make decisions or, are you always the one compromising (or getting your own way)?*

Name	Mutual Relationship	One-Sided *(you're doing the work)*	One-Sided *(they're doing the work)*	What Can You Do To Help?

Did anything surprise you after completing this exercise?

_____

_____

_____

_____

_____

What commitment can you make to yourself to nurture friendships and relationships that are the most satisfying?

___

Use this space to jot down any additional thoughts about the quality of your friendships and/or your qualities as a friend:

___

12 THE JOY OF ANCESTORS

My brother is a professor of religious studies and introduced me to a Mi'kmaq Elder from New Brunswick, Canada, that he had befriended along the way. I began helping their group with strategic planning around how to bring sweat lodge ceremonies to the United States, and attended several lodges myself as part of my healing journey. It was an incredible chance for me to grow and learn about myself and another culture.

As I was struggling about whether my marriage at the time could be saved, the Elder shared some great insight. He said that any unfinished business our ancestors had when they died, gets magnified and passed on to the next generation. One more time for emphasis: Any baggage our ancestors didn't deal with in their life time got magnified and passed on to my generation.

That's a heavy concept. I didn't know too much about my ancestors since many of them had already died when I was a young child. I was feeling pretty good about myself in general — although not as a relationship partner — so I figured that my then husband's family had left some heavy baggage behind. The Elder suggested a specific ceremony where you invite your ancestors to have a ceremonial feast with you, basically thank them for their participation, and ask them to release whatever baggage is still lurking. (Huge apologies to the Mi'kmaq for the way I butchered the description of this feast, but this is what I gleaned from what was explained to me.)

During the ceremony, I was convinced that I was participating for my husband's benefit – it wasn't going to be about me since I didn't have much baggage. Ha, the joke was on me!

Partway through the ceremony, I had an image of my paternal grandmother saying to me, "I made a mistake!" Given some lingering animosity between my Mom and this Grandmother several years prior, I was stunned. Was Grandma apologizing to all of us for being so harsh to my Mom about my brother Charlie's pending death? Was it that easy? If someone makes a mistake and owns it, is that's all that is needed to promote some serious ancestral healing? I had a sense that her spirit felt lighter and happier as a result of acknowledging her mistake.

It finally occurred to me that I had never truly allowed myself to make a mistake. Was it a mistake that I married this man? Could I just claim it, own it, and move on? Could we set each other free with no animosity? I suddenly felt so much lighter and free. I was able to let go of my fear of being labeled a two-time loser and move on. The healing at the "Dead Feast" was for ME! I wanted to stand at the top of a mountain and shout, "I made a mistake!" The sky wasn't going to fall in. It was a huge awakening for me – I could acknowledge that I made a mistake, own it, and move on. We ultimately decided to set each other free. I am forever grateful to that Elder and the community which helped me reclaim myself.

CHALLENGE ACTIVITY #12

As you think about your ancestors that have passed away as well as your relatives that are still alive, what potential baggage have they left behind that may be hindering you in ways you've never considered? Are there stories of unresolved conflict, challenges with alcohol or drugs, abandonment, etc., that may have been magnified and passed on to you and your loved ones? Think back on some of the stories — positive and negative — that you've heard over the years to see what may be lingering. You may be stuck in a pattern leftover from them.

List anything you can remember that might be playing out in your life today. In addition to obvious concerns (i.e., if you have an ancestor that struggled with substance use disorder you have a genetic predisposition to having substance use disorder yourself), also include things that are on an "energy" level. Remember that you can't change what's unconscious until you make it conscious. Reach out and gather more information if you need to!

The great news that the Elder shared is that the healing that can happen through the ceremonial feast impacts not only the ancestor that left the baggage behind, but every ancestor in between from that time period forward.

Jot down things that might be lingering from your ancestors.

Relationship	**Maternal**	**Paternal**
Parents		
Grandparents		
Great Grandparents		
Anyone farther back?		

How can you best release the leftover baggage from generations back to ensure you can move forward in your life free from their leftover stuff? Not everyone has access to a Native American Elder. Consider finding a quiet space in your house or in nature that has meaning to you, perhaps light a candle and meditate. Ask your ancestors to show themselves to you and ask them if they have any regrets of things that they've done or left undone while they were here on earth. See what bubbles up for you and capture it below. Don't worry about whether it's just in your mind, your subconscious or maybe a visitation from a spirit. I think that any information you get is valid for your journey.

List the themes and ideas that bubbled up during your meditation below. How might they be impacting your happiness in your life today?

Theme/Idea	How Might This Impact Me?

Did any new nuggets or thoughts get raised for you in doing this exercise?

_____

_____

_____

_____

_____

_____

13 RECLAIM YOUR POWER AND GIVE IT AWAY

Power is a tricky thing... people sometimes crave it while others run from it. We inadvertently give it away, or hug it so close that it can't be taken away from us. Hearing the phrase, "S/he who has the most power is the one who gives it away" gave me a new perspective. My journey started with learning how to respect myself, to set boundaries so I didn't feel taken advantage of, and to identify my own goals and dreams to help give me focus independent from any loved ones.

A work-related consultant told me once, "You're working way harder than you need to!" In my insecurity, I felt like I needed to have all the answers. I thought that my staff and board were looking to me to be the expert. What they really wanted (and needed) was to be included in problem-solving and planning discussions so they could have a sense of ownership of our mission and programs. Once I could translate that into my daily work life, I could breathe easier and put more energy into helping to grow the people around me. I now surround myself with brilliant people and try to feed off of each other's energy.

Years ago my fellowship group was invited to do some consulting at Dartmouth College. I specifically remember freaking out to the fellowship director about how I wasn't an expert. I was stressing about what skills I had that I could offer to people at Dartmouth. Dartmouth? I was from New Hampshire and was keenly aware of Dartmouth's reputation.

She chuckled at me, clearly amused at my anxiety and intimidation about the prestige of folks at Dartmouth. She gently replied, "Being an expert is NOT having all of the answers. It's about knowing what questions to ask." Whoa... I was great at asking questions! I never made assumptions about things. Maybe I could feel comfortable going to Dartmouth and asking pointed questions to help people come to their own discoveries. I began to imagine that maybe, just maybe, I was enough of an question-asking expert to be helpful!

When my daughter was getting ready to go to college, I knew I needed a new way to channel all of my Mom energy, so I took a glass-melting class and started my own business called Empty Nest Glassworks. I spent about eight years hand-melting glass beads for handles of salad sets, bottle openers, wine stoppers, etc. and selling them at craft shows. The funny part is when I was designing my business cards I struggled with whether I could call myself a Lampwork Artist. Who gets to decide whether I'm an artist or not? There was no secret society of people that would judge me fit to call myself an artist. No licensure or exam to pass. Could I just declare that it was so? Apparently YES. I could and I did. But the struggle was important. I'm experiencing the same battle now that I'm writing this. Can I actually declare myself an author? Apparently YES I can.

Never be afraid to chase your dream, to live your life fully and to declare it so. Every single one of us has unique gifts to give to the world. It is our responsibility to identify them, develop them — whatever they may be — and then find a way to share them with the rest of the world.

CHALLENGE ACTIVITY #13

Are there parts of yourself that you hold on to out of fear? What would happen if you reclaim your personal power and declare it so? I still struggle with the awkward balance between being really humble and being really confident in who I am. Sharing so deeply of myself is really scary, but if one person — out of the dozen who might read this — feels a sense of hope for their future, then it's been worth it to me.

List the things that you still struggle with to live a fully authentic life:

_____

_____

_____

_____

_____

_____

_____

_____

_____

What (baby) steps can you take going forward to grow closer to sharing your amazing self with the world? What's the worst thing that could happen if you do that? Start with the people you trust to keep your heart safe as you share more deeply with others. Being vulnerable is really hard, but in the long run, is the only way to fully live.

_____

_____

_____

_____

_____

_____

_____

_____

_____

_____

_____

WHAT'S NEXT?

Once you find your authentic self, through your own self-reflection and through completing some of these activities, it's a whole other challenge to balance everything while being in a relationship. Stay tuned for my next workbook about living authentically in a relationship with another person. As of this writing, I'm 12 years into an incredible relationship with the love of my life. When he proposed, I burst into tears and told him, "I guarantee I'm going to ruin your life." After he replied, "I'm okay with that..." I jumped in headfirst to planning our 2012 wedding. It was worth struggling with two failed marriages to have arrived where I am today. Don't give up. The journey is worth it!

ABOUT THE AUTHOR

Betsy Houde has served as executive director of The Youth Council in Nashua, New Hampshire since 1996. She has been recognized locally and throughout New Hampshire for innovative programming and extensive collaboration developing numerous programs serving children, teens and families. In 2002, Betsy was named one of 10 people across the country awarded a 3-year fellowship with the Robert Wood Johnson Foundation to develop leadership skills in reducing substance misuse. Betsy was named one of Greater Nashua's 25 Extraordinary Women in 2013, and has received several other state and local honors.

Betsy served as a founding board member of the Endowment for Health, and was a 12-year member of the NH Governor's Commission on Alcohol and Drug Abuse Prevention, Intervention and Treatment. Today Betsy consults with Nashua Prevention Coalition, Merrimack Safeguard, NH Juvenile Court Diversion Network and serves on many local boards throughout the City of Nashua.

A New London, Connecticut native, Betsy received her Bachelor of Arts degree from Connecticut College in 1983 double majoring in Child Development and Sociology-Based Human Relations and a Master of Arts in Counseling with distinction from Rivier College in 1990. An active member of the Rotary Club of Nashua West, Betsy was honored to serve as president in 2013-2014. Formerly known as Betsy Abrahams, Betsy changed her name to Houde after her 2012 marriage.

Betsy can be reached at BetsyHoude@gmail.com.

Made in the USA
Columbia, SC
22 July 2018